# Waking Up
### to the
# Pattern Left
### by a
# Snail Overnight

# Waking Up
## to the
# Pattern Left
## by a
# Snail Overnight

*Poems*

**JIM PASCUAL AGUSTIN**

Published by Gaudy Boy LLC,
an imprint of Singapore Unbound
www.singaporeunbound.org/gaudyboy
New York

For more information on ordering books, contact
jkoh@singaporeunbound.org.

ISBN 978-1-958652-00-8

Cover design by Flora Chan
Interior design by Jennifer Houle

*For Kiara, Nina*
*& Margie*

# Contents

## *bound by wood*

My Mother Had a Concrete Garden     1
Waking Up to the Pattern Left by a Snail Overnight     2
Entangled     3
The Tin     5
Containing Light     6
Light and Rain     7
Curl of a Rescue Cat     8
Ant Garden     12
Sometimes It's Better Not Knowing     13
Inosculation     14
Chameleon on the Ground a Few Feet from
    a Tree We Walk Past Every Day     15
The World is Round as a Drop of Water     16
Masked Days     17
Light Attaches to a Girl     18
The Struggle for Water     19
You're Only a Number Now     20

## *the belly of a termite*

The Name of the Land is One     23
We Danced with Strangers     24
Amorsolo's "Tinikling in Barrio"     25
Lecaroz's "Bamboo Dancing"     26
Fingertips     27
For the Saviors     28
Wall and Candle     29

Ear of Wax                                              30
For Maria Ressa                                         32
The Mad Man as President                                33
Photograph in the Rain                                  34
The Soft Criminal                                       35
After Seeing *Mad Max: Fury Road*                       36
Dissonance                                              37

## *something in its grip*

Correspondence                                          41
Discord                                                 42
No Past, No Future                                      43
I Never Know Where I Am with You                        44
Door in the Dark                                        45
Concern                                                 46
Kaze No Denwa                                           47
My Body Remembered What My Mind Forgot                  49
Vinegar Eyes                                            50
Dancing with a Phantom Limb                             51
I Keep Hoping These are Just Bad Dreams a
    Toe Can Shake Off                                   52
Leaving the Infinite Library                            53
The Bound and the Free                                  54
Keeping Busy as the World Spins Itself Hollow           55
Departure                                               56
Ashes                                                   57
The Same Jewels                                         60
The Box                                                 61
Dry Bones                                               62

## resonate
### a series of poems after a line mis/heard from Björk's "Anchor Song"

Enduring the Night                      65

Injuring the Night                      66

Injuring the Knight                     67

Injured in the Night                    68

And You Ring the Night                  69

And You're in the Night                 70

End During the Night                    71

And During the Night                    72


*Acknowledgments & Some Notes*          75

*About the Author*                      77

*About Gaudy Boy*                       79

# Waking Up
## to the
# Pattern Left
## by a
# Snail Overnight

# bound by wood

# My Mother Had a Concrete Garden

Pots she gathered of different shapes
and state, some cracked, some battered,
all unwanted. And past the concrete
roads, far from where the government
stabbed the names of politicians in poles,
she found soil that could hold
young shoots begging
to be nurtured. And this she did
in silence, people thought she was mute.
But she hummed in the absence
of an audience, in the hope a single leaf
would push out of handfuls of soil.
I was too impatient and missed
when light green unexpectedly
made her gasp.

# Waking Up to the Pattern Left by a Snail Overnight

Troubled as a dream
without an end.
It is all water
and glass, this world
bound by wood,
not knowing it
was a window.

# Entangled

*for Kiara Silayan*

We scrambled among the rocks in search
of a picnic spot. Our chatter mingling
with the relentless waves. Then, nearly dropping
a piece of melon, you stood up in sudden panic
shouting, "Something touched my leg!"

We shrugged it off as seaweed,
and then it happened again.
A form hiding under the rock
you were sitting on undulated
into a question mark: the bubbled limb
of an octopus, irate at our intrusion.

You moved to another spot, wishing
we could find another pool. We hushed away
your worries with soft laughter.
The sun crossed the sky, and to your relief,
we packed up and started back to the hut.

You dug nails into the sides
of your little bag,
your fingers entangled
in its narrow straps.

Then from among the boulders a seagull
came down with a screech
and scooped up with its deep scarlet beak
that soft and spineless thing you feared.

3

In the air they struggled,
one shape, though clearly two,
stretching those few seconds
into a rubber band
until the snap.

# The Tin

A cousin whose father had gone to work overseas came to our door,
laughing. His family received a parcel; he wanted to show me
the gift he got for Christmas. It was only November.

He giggled before he took out a small tin, like that for baked beans.
It had a plastic net and bright colors, with a button to activate the toy.
His eyes grew wide as he clicked it. He flipped the tin upside down,
and it let out the sound of a cow mooing as it shuddered in his hand.
We laughed. He flipped it again.

It went on for a while. Until finally I wondered how many more times
the cow would keep mooing before it grew hoarse and tired.
I looked inside our house. My father was helping my mother
cut up scraps of vegetables for supper without looking at each other,
tossing pieces into the deep frying pan that sizzled. The smoke
clouded their eyes. My cousin knew he had to go.

# Containing Light

### 1

Science and commerce keep trying to find ways
to contain light, measure its immensity, trace
its trajectories and many lives. To capture it
as if it were a beast, harness its mysteries
like any other commodity.

They would do well to ask trees.

### 2

What is a simple wooden coffin but the body
of a tree reduced to panels of measured dimensions?
Skinned and stripped, it bears little resemblance
to what it was when life pulsed through its core,
running from limb to limb, all the way
to the slenderest roots and most ragged ends
of leaves.

It is easy to forget how trees,
with murmuring fingers,
gather light and water to the deep darkness
of their cores. Silently they perform
what in another realm
would be called magic.

# Light and Rain

The mountain, a shape suddenly darker
than the skies that mask the time of day.
It would be so much easier to surrender
the mind to the limits of the body,
let frustration rub
against the nearest stranger.

But then a giggle from a little girl
pricks my ears. I turn to her.
"Mama, look at the lights!" She is tugging
at a woman who has fallen close to sleep.
An orange globe rests in the girl's
left hand as she points with her right.

The woman shifts out of slumber.
"The lights are clinging to the windows!
They look like my naartjie!" Laughing,
the girl digs her thumbs into the fruit,
releases in such a small and crowded space
more than just a scent.

# Curl of a Rescue Cat

Stray kitten, cobweb-
like, clinging on the wire gate.
Fell out Santa's bag.

Mother cat lost track
of you, little injured one.
Throb of fur, my palm.

Eyes dull as spilt milk
on the floor, you sniff yourself
a shrivelled corner.

A silver bowl nudged
near your corner. Eyes askance,
food, drink. A trap. Trust.

Darting in matted
forest of fur, fleeting specks
we need to murder.

We lost a cat once,
to dogs or electric fence.
Not again. Stay home.




Clacking teeth, muffled
meows. Lonesome greetings to birds
on the other side.




Kiara taught you claws
can unlatch windows open.
A nudge. Freedom. Fear.

One escape, something
sent you clawing up a tree.
Shivering fur ball.

Curl of cat, my lap
a bed only when needed.
So purrs summer's end.

# Ant Garden

Pincers measure shards of leaves
licked and laid in layers, a living bed
of cut emeralds. Here they gather seeds
of epiphytes that may one day unfurl
their scents like invisible banners.

Ant antennae of different species gather,
waving in communion, forgetting all enmity.
With murmurs, they coax slender roots
to wrap around the host tree,
nurture young sprouts to rise sunward.

With limbs thin as needles, they resist
the drag of wind and rain. As one,
they weave leaf by leaf a symphony
of whispers high up in the trees,
a garden of secret hymns.

# Sometimes It's Better Not Knowing

Eyes, go roll away on your own
in search of sockets that belong
to no one. For there are no more
skies that bear clouds. The leaves
have abandoned all trees.
And the swings in all playgrounds
will never be disturbed by tiny hands.
The chains that bind are all gone
the way of all elements exposed
to what devours them.

# Inosculation

First there is only the sound of leaves
from either tree that trails the passing breeze.

Two trees, separate in their long search
in the darkness of the soil and the light

far above, finally find that moment of touch.
A branch catching the other's, a root

like a nervous finger, or their sides
slowly pushed together by constant wind,

the need for more room to grow.
Then it happens. Once solitary skins

begin to sense each other past resistance.
A bond, a union, woven in silence.

# Chameleon on the Ground a Few Feet from a Tree We Walk Past Every Day

Toes fused to stillness,
no memory of the pendulum gait
before gripping a branch.
Once-swivelling eyes
now stare a permanent grey
on concrete corroded by rain.

Tongue curled inward,
the reverse of a hiss.
Cardboard-flat, stiff
from head to tail, the missing
puzzle piece of a tree.

# The World is Round as a Drop of Water

The drought may choke
the bordered land,
but one day rain
will soften even
the tips of barbed wire.

# Masked Days

The reporter on the radio
is not given a list of the names
of those who died overnight.
She reads through the static
the breakdown of the numbers.

Those who still can, breathe
through filters the next day,
weary of restrictions and distances,
the unseen enemy likely, lingering
in the air, on the skin of things
they dread to touch.

Are we lucky to hope
to remember today, instead
of being remembered?

Meanwhile, on an abandoned beach,
there is a bag of sand
collected and tied into a bundle
by a child who had to flee.
The bag grows heavy
with every wave
but can only stay.

# Light Attaches to a Girl

*"All at once you look across a crowded room*
*To see the way that light attaches to a girl."*
—"A Long December," Counting Crows

This little girl may one day forget
that wedding day, the flowing white dress,
the numbered guests, the flowers
she held on instruction.
She may not remember how the wind
blew her hair, how the light touched her skin,
how she ran with the other girls
when they forgot
why they were there at all,
wearing masks that muffled their laughter.

And in those brief moments,
a veil is lifted, a shadow shed.
The world cannot end.

# The Struggle for Water

Turn the tap. Add a smile, pretend
you're twisting the ear of the school bully.
Some taps you don't even touch,
convenient, much safer for times like these.
Soap and water for at least 20 seconds,
that's how you wash away the virus,
they say. But they forget
not everyone has a tap.

To others, thirst knocks on the door
before dawn touches the roof
of the hut. The buckets echo
the last crickets.

The way to the river is marked
by reading which beast left
droppings or faint footprints.
And once the shores of the narrowing
river are reached, one has to learn to listen
as the buckets are filled.
Teeth. Claws.
More real
than any virus.

# You're Only a Number Now

Don't squirm. I'm just putting you in a parcel
without a stamp or return address,
sending you back to where nightmares are born.

Suck at the tattered ends of your umbilical cord,
soothe yourself as we curse you on your way.
You never gave us a chance to say goodbye
to the ones we love. Ash is just not the same.

You forced us to inhale what we exhale,
to be aware of the distance
we have to keep if we wanted to live
another day.

# the belly of a termite

# The Name of the Land is One

The name of the land is one
of many claims.
It matters less who first set foot
on its tumbling shores and jagged cliffs,
who first tore branches
from silent trees to light a fire
for warmth or to drive away
the lurking darkness.

The deadly dance of shadows
and dreams never left the faces
of mute rocks. The pages
of history books are scarred
with endless accounts
by victors who burned
what they could not bear.

The name of the land
is less worthy than the air
where birds have dominion.
Tell me, do fish see straight lines
in the waters? Do hooves
heed hand-drawn borders
or the seasons?

# We Danced with Strangers

Laughter and the touch of strangers
are what I remember most that night,
moments before the old year gave way
to the new. We danced in circles intoxicated
not with alcohol, but with something that had
nothing to do with the past.

My brown arms grew sweaty as they rubbed
against someone else's, someone I had just met
by chance. Our eyes reflected the flash
of colors in that dim tavern.

Rage Against the Machine
took turns with Lionel Richie
and Earth Wind and Fire.

It was the year Mandela never saw coming
while he was in prison, though he must have dreamed it
countless times when the lights went out,
or as he struck a rhythm from a boulder
with a state-issued hammer.

# Amorsolo's "Tinikling in Barrio"

Bamboo thicker than limbs, bowing
and rising to the will and the weight

of the wind. Who thought of cutting
them down, laying them on the ground

to keep a rhythm? Slow and building,
frantic and threatening,

a dance only for the daring
and nimble of feet. The crush

of a crowd, the village elite,
a celebration of the bounty.

A scene suffused with light,
it is easy to forget

what lies in the shadows
of the looming church behind.

# Lecaroz's "Bamboo Dancing"

In this dance, our feet must stay
with the rhythm of bamboo.

Always together, always in keeping
with the rise and fall.

We hold each other for common balance,
letting go only to add a flourish.

Not a bead of sweat
shows on our foreheads,

the pace in our hearts
we keep to ourselves.

Just for this performance, we own
the ground where we barely stand.

# Fingertips

I have lost the lines on my fingertips
many times through the years.
From touching the sides
of something hot and metallic,
from clinging too long
when I should have let go,
or from needing to slice
layers off that had gone stuck
with instant glue.

I can no longer confirm if my father
ever warmed the trigger among strangers.
I was too young to ask then
why he was going out
to sow fear in the guise of order,
in the name of the dictator
who would one day die in exile.
The dictator was no saint, was never
untouchable like they all believed.

Those were dark times
even as these are dark times.
Our shadows, our own.
My sisters say my resemblance
to him grows stronger by the day.
Yet we do not live sharing
the same breath. I keep my distance
to survive for fear of the virus
that has struck so many down.
I rarely go out,
touch others even less.

# For the Saviors

I can now walk on the side of the road
without having to avoid traces
of blood or the shadows of the murdered.

At home I no longer need to bolt
the windows shut, fearing
the creeping voices of prisoners.

Freedom is so visible, it makes the eyes
of babies look like wounds
while the newspapers declare the names

of the new saviors of the land.

# Wall and Candle

Grown-ups spoke in whispers as if someone
in the shadows were standing, waiting for a name
or location or anything random. A fragment of truth,
a hint of dissent. And what are children
if not armed with curiosity, poking at the borders
of what's allowed, what's forbidden?

Then one of us found a candle. Though broken
at the middle, it could still be stabbed to stand
on its own melted foot. Against the wall, a fist
is a boulder or an egg about to crack.
Unclenched, our hands could take on any form.
Our fingers spread into eagle wings.
Elephants swung their trunks, dogs and ducks
shattered the imposed silence.

We laughed without asking permission.

# Ear of Wax

*On the clandestine burial of the late Philippine dictator,*
*Ferdinand Marcos, 18 November 2016*

Ear of wax
forehead of wax
lips and nose of wax
cheeks of wax
fingers without bones
torso without a spine
hair from someone else
that resembled what was once
the only crown you can rightly claim.

It matters little, the authenticity
of whatever remains were stuffed
in the box, hastily shoved in ground
not meant for pretend
heroes with genuine guile.

Guinness-stamped post-World War II
king of plunderers, drone-voiced singer
to a single broken-winged dove, commander
of troops that delivered eternal silence
and disappearances, I would love to see you
turn in your grave (wherever that really is).

Those who announce
their love for the scraps
of the legacy you left behind
thought they had succeeded
in stopping us
from setting you alight.

# For Maria Ressa

Like spiders weaving traps through the night,
there are those who wish you grow wings
small and fragile as a butterfly's.

How sad to see their flimsy limbs
bobbing among stark branches
of trees long abandoned by leaves.

Even as the sun rises, now
they pull and drag almost unseen
webs from their sore asses.

# The Mad Man as President

He uses a hammer to crush
stains on the shirts he wears.

With hands trembling
and a plastered laugh
hyenas cannot hide,
he pounds semen, blood,
fragments of bone again
and again until they blend
into a pattern.

Broadcast live nationwide
what normally was performed
in secret, this act so awed millions
of captive minds, they handed him
the highest throne of the land.

Years later, he still flaunts
the same clothes, dances
with the same hammer.
But his old swing has gone the way
of drunks, bears a grimace
when he ends up hitting
his own head and groin.

# Photograph in the Rain

*for Leni Robredo*


Years ago, a stranger took that photo of you from the back
without asking your permission, posted it
on social media where I heard of you for the first time.

I'd been away for decades, but I recognized
those skies, rinsing the pollution in the air
that builds up again the following morning.

It seemed nothing more then than the picture of a woman
in the rain holding an umbrella against Manila's grim
evening. Plain shirt and jeans, a small shoulder bag.
You stood alone near a corner, waiting for a bus.

Not a car with a dedicated driver. No bodyguard
in sight. A seat in Congress but patiently waiting
for a ride home, like most of us,
in shoes that couldn't get more wet.

# The Soft Criminal

*"The law is soft on criminals"*

—JACOB ZUMA, 21 FEBRUARY 2021

A termite is a slave to the scent
of wood. It is unable to resist the temptation
to carve what it craves until it grows
hollow. Though it churns what once was stiff
and towering, the belly of a termite remains soft.
A bathtub of milk is a faint comparison.

In a homestead where the only firepool in the world
lies, Jacob Zuma dreams of floating in milk
as he laughs. He doesn't know that the milk is made
from crushed termites. Their tiny legs
and broken pincers, curved and straight in places,
begin to form letters and numbers. They cling
to his limbs. He tries desperately to shake them off,
clawing at his own skin. Suddenly he remembers
how to bleed.

# After Seeing *Mad Max: Fury Road*

In this world, water is a womb on a citadel
of rock. There is a mad frenzy in the air.
People move like spiders, climbing nearly vertical
walls, even the children are not children,
but remnants of old clothes stitched together.
There's a crunch of sand between the teeth
if anyone ever tries to speak.

The women stay silent, a rusty dagger
hidden between folds of skin.
Max, stray as a muzzled dog, dangles
on protruding lengths of metal.
In the crush of rock and steel, something
is bound to be broken, a chain,
a twisted order. Something else
without yet a name will become flesh.

# Dissonance

Like a scene from a sci-fi B movie, the door opened,
and ground crew, without protective suits, bustled in
to spray the cabin. Through the sudden cloud, I saw
seagulls at a nearby dump, their throats close to bursting
as they screeched at each other, fighting over
what another species had discarded.

This was my first view of Africa
nearly 30 years ago, a stopover before Jo'burg.
No different from an alien from another galaxy,
another time. Only later would I learn
of others from my home country, survivors
of shipwrecks more than a century ago.
They established the first fishing community
near the bottom of the continent. But though we came
from the same troubled archipelago, I had never caught
a single fish. I'm far less equipped to catch one
than a seagull. How can I even claim a distant kinship?

My skin not quite dark enough and far
from white. Some might say the documents
I earned are nothing but lies. My children
did not choose their mixed parentage, yet they suffer
the randomness of hate when I am not there
to defend them. I can still hear those seagulls
circling, tearing at the air with their screams,
laying claim to what was once someone else's.

# *something in its grip*

# Correspondence

To be made to feel without a light
the inside of a box with walls
bristling with thorns. The stomach
of a manufactured beast that feeds
on anger and loneliness. My shoe
when I was a little boy in a jeepney,
the one that no adult noticed
got left behind. How I worried
about getting my white sock dirty.

# Discord

A palm reader once told me not to believe
everything she might say. "In utter darkness,
you sense only what's in reach. With fingertips
for eyes, what feels like the handle of a spoon
may be a knife; a waft of warm air, the breath
of a murderer." She traced my palms
as if they were the walls of a cave.

Wanting to test her patience and claimed skill,
I was tempted to ask her to look at my knuckles
instead, but she gave me the stare of someone
drowning by choice as fog coiled over the skin
of a lake without a name. So I bit my tongue
close to bleeding, and let her murmur
the nonsense I paid for and expected.

"Your generation was birthed in discord,
my child of so few moons. Here is the line
that forks, though you only see a single path
on your journey. Your heart, a fist without walls
to pound. You must learn to listen
through the drone of your own slumber.
There will be a burning you will have to bear.
Remember who lives and who dies
when you finally rise from the ashes
of departure."

Her booth, a wooden box
with rust stains on the door, little more
than an upright coffin. I don't know how
she knew I was leaving.

# No Past, No Future

Your palms react and retract
from the touch of my hand,
as if they had been scraped
by a bad fall. We often fail
to notice the sharpness of a blade
on the ground where we stand,
the ground we walk each day.
It is easy to forget that sometimes
it is necessary to go slowly
or come to a complete stop
when there is thick fog or hard rain
or when smoke engulfs us, billowing
from a fire that cannot be traced.

# I Never Know Where I Am with You

A car swerves from its lane,
pushed by a wind blast
or a giant hand
legible as God's writing.

The driver loses control, turns the wheel
from side to side, desperately trying
to guess the direction furthest
from ending up tangled in a puzzle
of rubber, glass, and steel.

You know I'm not talking
about safe driving. We navigate
the world's most fatal streets.
You turn away, eyes and ears
numb to me.

# Door in the Dark

What used to be a tree
was measured and cut to fit
a frame that left no room
for leaves. Leaving and arriving
became its only dream.

This light in the kitchen
cast the unoccupied room
in a shape I never saw
before. Though upright,
it recalled something
that had to be
lowered into the ground.

What else could the silent
darkening of a teabag
in a cup conjure
an hour past midnight?

# Concern

At an angle and force unexpected, the severed end
of a branch thicker than my arm touched my leg
as I stood at a dump site unloading garden prunings.

Made me pause in the grabbing and tossing
upon a rising mound a few meters away
from the swinging of an earth mover's
metallic teeth. I winced.

Today I look at the scabbing wound, a brown-red
spot, nearly perfectly round. My mind crawls back
in time: my mother's hands tending my aching palms
after a bad fall, my father watching, so heavy with concern
he almost cried.

# Kaze No Denwa

*When Itaru Sasaki lost his cousin in 2010, he decided to build a glass-paneled phone booth in his hilltop garden with a disconnected rotary phone inside for communicating with his lost relative, to help him deal with his grief.*

*Only a year later, Japan faced the horrors of a triple disaster: an earthquake followed by a tsunami, which caused a nuclear meltdown. Sasaki's coastal hometown of Otsuchi was hit with 30-foot waves. Ten percent of the town died in the flood. Sasaki opened his kaze no denwa or "wind phone" to the now huge number of people in the community mourning the loss of loved ones. Eventually word spread and others experiencing grief made the pilgrimage from around the country.*

—"Wind Telephone," *Atlas Obscura*

When I have time and money, I won't go to Japan
to climb a hill outside a city where a glass-paneled
phone booth waits for words of grief to pour
out of me. I will not be a boulder cracked by water
that has finally found its way out of darkness.

I can understand those who take the trip, changing trains
at stations far out of their daily routes. Perhaps tourists
from other countries, not just locals, may wind
their way to that hill. An anime story in real life.
But money is a luxury, travel never free except on foot.

Instead, I will stay where I am, on the other side
of the world from where my parents are buried.
The long drought has parched the field. A fire awaits
should lightning strike. A broken bottle partly hidden
and the fierce sun at the perfect angle could spark a flame.

My parents can visit me in my dreams
while I inhale the distant sea air
that may somehow reach the veld. They won't
taunt me for my absence, for not even
choosing the words on their tombstones.

# My Body Remembered What My Mind Forgot

Ill at ease, a lone ant
that has lost the scent.

In the corner of my eye,
a shadow without a shape
but always lingering.

The troubled slumber of a beast
that must wait for the sun's turning
as it wears its loosened skin.

The next day, a short message
from my sister flies across the seas,
reaches me in an instant.

Today is the anniversary
of my father's death.

# Vinegar Eyes

Before the procession,
adults would lift children over the casket
to spare them visits from the newly departed.
The men spun the coffin in circles
as the women wept and wailed.
So much movement and noise to disorient
the spirit, prevent it from lingering
among the living. Then everyone washes
their eyes with vinegar. Death, a wound
exposed in the sun. Rituals I remember
from my country of birth.

Now in another country, I fumble
with knots on plastic bags of clothes.
The paper skin of cardboard boxes
stick as I rip off packaging tape.
Personal possessions spill
under the fluorescent stare,
to be sorted through the night.
Which to keep,
which to pass on to strangers
or hurl in the garbage bin.
After everything is done,
how does one hold
a box of ash?

# Dancing with a Phantom Limb

You laughed when you saw your hand try to scratch
the back of a knee that was no longer there.
My smile was a late and uncomfortable response.

The rest of your body swerved as if to deliver a kick
to a soccer ball that strayed toward us. We watched it
continue rolling past where your foot should have been.

Once you shuddered without warning, as if an exposed
electric cable had touched your leg, the one they had to sever
in an attempt to stop the cancer.

That beast, detected by instruments that traced
only what gets ravaged, played random games with your flesh,
drained the glimmer in your eyes at unexpected moments.

If I had known then how much you loved to dance,
I would have asked you to show me your best moves,
perhaps use my shoulder for balance.

A pair with three legs, laughing away
the awkwardness and the pain, as if we had known
each other since childhood and the day wouldn't end.

# I Keep Hoping These are Just Bad Dreams a Toe Can Shake Off

We are wounds, eyes that bleed
to see the world, lips that murmur
prayers no religion can teach.
You never said any of that, it's just me
imagining you did, again and again
when you look away.

I turn into a mute child
on a raft as flimsy as shredded
newspaper. It won't be long
before it closes up like a wilted
flower and swallows my silence.

In time we grow tough as eternal scabs,
repeatedly pried open and dried.
Our separate and unreleased
lamentations howling inside.

# Leaving the Infinite Library

It would be her last visit before she turns the key the other direction. In her transparent bag, lit up with the reflection of the walls which concealed automated eyes, a book she had searched a lifetime. She knew who might be watching her, and she tried her best to show how little she cared what they thought.

That book, no one else could read and truly understand. It was bound to look like any other book in that library, bound with material from a placenta reconstituted by a spinning process that resembled a loom. It was the same placenta that carried her first moments in the womb. As she approached the exit which was also the only way in, a device the size of her hand swung toward her and pricked her right index finger. A final confirmation. Then the librarian appeared on the panel before her.

"Infinity is but a moment here. You know that once you read that book there is no turning back, my child?"

She nodded. She could already recall the first scent of blood that came rushing out of her: warmth, surprise, fear.

# The Bound and the Free

The gate left open,
a single wing,
droplets of rain
for feathers.

Fortune's dark twin
has always lurked in the corner
of my eye, waiting to pounce
at the slightest hint
of hesitation in my breath,
that inevitable misstep.

Soundtrack: frantic violins
at high pitch, one can almost see
strings snapping, flailing
in arcs like someone's long hair
whose body cannot control
its trajectory.

The slow easing of a screw
by patient penetration of rain
and rust. A petal slipping
into the gap under the door
to escape the Southeaster.

Whatever happens next
will bind itself
to my shadow.

# Keeping Busy as the World
# Spins Itself Hollow

A branch swayed by the breeze
becomes a small hand tapping
at the window. The kettle on the counter
rattles the cup that had long lost
its matching saucer. For a moment,
I turn away from what must be done.

I struggle with the tough skin
of a butternut that resists
the peeler's blade. A few strokes
at different angles does the trick.
Bright yellow strips begin to scatter
around the chopping board.

I do not scoop out the core
where the slimy seeds lie,
for the deep orange veins
are stuck tight to the round walls.
I take a knife and cut around
that ovary-shaped hiding place.

Surrounded by yellow-orange
geometric pieces, wreathed by strands
of sunlight, the shape in the center collapses.
Only then do I begin to tremble.

# Departure

I drove over 30 kilometers in the dark
to where you last answered my calls.
I pounded. Silence behind the door.

Later, the rummaging through
the familiar that seemed
suddenly a stranger's.

The clothes you wore,
the shoes with dust
embedded in the soles,

the discarded cellphone
in the drawer full
of twisted cables.

The spout of the shaving cream
still tipped with foam. The razor
with fine lines of hair. Runes.

# Ashes

1

My father's ash tray, a mechanical wonder
for a child in the 70s. Awed,
I watched him press the stick in the middle
that set a disc under a cross of metal
spinning like a frantic toy
until ash and cigarette butts
were swallowed in a rattle
of cylindrical darkness.

When no one was around,
I dismantled that gadget, releasing
a shower of gray and stench
all over my clothes, my face.

**2**

A shopping bag can hold so many things
as long as its plastic skin
isn't punctured. This came to mind
when I saw a series of photos
taken by a friend who covered
the first days of COVID-19
in the Philippines. A woman cradling
such a bag in her arms, leaving
the crematorium on foot.

My friend gave her and her family a ride
because no one would.
And all I could think of was that bag,
the weight, the possibility of bursting.

### 3

Yesterday was the birthday of my mother-in-law
who died a month ago. We took some of her ashes
to her house at nightfall, secretly scattered them
in the garden so the tenants wouldn't know.
One of our daughters volunteered.
She calmly walked next to the fence
where the branches of the frangipani
spread out, a network of bone.
The wild dagga covered her shape
from the view of the windows.

It took her a while to untie
the sandwich bag my wife had prepared,
a mixture of ash and flowers.
My daughter waved when she finally emptied
the packet while my wife and I watched
in the car. It felt like being in a bad spy movie,
we couldn't help laughing.

# The Same Jewels

*You wear the same jewels*
*That I gave you*
*As you bury me*
    —TAYLOR SWIFT, "MY TEARS RICOCHET"

The dogs are barking at nothing again. Perhaps at the wind that tugs
at the leaves ahead of their due falling. Maybe dead stars stab the eyes
of the dogs as they look up sniffing in the expanding shadows.

I could never read the minds of other people's dogs, could never see
past their teeth. One researcher said they can sense bad people,
or at least something close to rotting. As if none of us is forever
on the boundaries of corruption, a turning to carbon and other elements
beyond the measure of science. A con sometimes, science,
in the hands of those who trust instruments above the unseen
and immeasurable. The few grams between the last breath and after.

You and I, for all we claim to know, could be nothing but jewels
in someone else's trinket box. A box lugged around, shaken,
easily lost and forgotten in a dark corner, only remembered
at random by a being far beyond our reckoning. A box, a coffin.

I'm sure the dogs can hear me singing in my head
as I walk past the fence that keeps them in, singing to fight
the trembling as they snarl and snap at my swinging limbs.
The first departed to be afraid of another living thing.

# The Box

The box, narrow enough to hold
three cigars cut short.
An odd comparison. You never smoked
apart from weed that made you laugh.

We opened that box
at the top of a hill you used to hike.
We meant to let your ash
take to the breeze.
But one never sees
where the wind goes
until it shakes something in its grip.

And so it happened, you swirled
for a while then curled
back to our faces
when we expected you
to be taken away.
Got a powdery taste
of your remains.
Suddenly aged, our only response
between tears
was uncontrollable laughter.

# Dry Bones

Ezekiel saw a version of *The Walking Dead*
in reverse. In the Valley of Dry Bones,
worms wither as they empty
their bellies. Ligaments stitch
joints together. The last breath
becomes the first, just before
final words sound like an infant's
initial cry.

If I were Ezekiel, I would have fled
into a cave or a distant hill.
Perhaps that is what separates me
from all the prophets, false or real.
I have no stomach
for vivid visions or gods
who play favorites
among those they claim to love.

When my jaws open
for the last time, leave them be.
Let the worms keep
what they have to take from me.

# resonate:
## a series of poems after a line mis/heard from Björk's "Anchor Song"

# Enduring the Night

When he saw the moon sketch
outlines on the ground, he wished
for a time machine and a past

before people believed doors, walls,
roofs, and windows kept them safe
from what lurks outside, free and untamed.

How does one endure sleeping
in a house where only ashes quiver,
nudged by a draft that slips past
through slender gaps, gropes
along passages of brick and cement?

The bed, a chasm that could never be crossed
in daylight or when night eventually falls.
The homeless must not forget their luck.
A ceiling of stars is not for everyone.

# Injuring the Night

Injuring the night's skin, boots
dark with someone else's blood.

Shattering the night's skull, porcelain
cups the shape of babies' mouths.

Twisting the night's spine, dawn
throwing ropes of light.

# Injuring the Knight

Magellan, in salt-dulled armor clanging
before a weathered cross,
thought he'd pacify the seas
with his trusted sword.

But the tropical sun struck his head,
the rising tide coiled and curled
around his legs.

The natives saw
that injuring the knight
meant finding points of weakness
in the clumsy metal.
A poisoned arrow tip and a sharp eye,
a flailing of blades in unison.

Magellan charted his own
watery end and fed
the local fish population.
Too late to learn how the sea
seals its wounds after each cutting.

# Injured in the Night

*for Joel Pablo Salud*


September is a war of memories
in the home country. Roads and alleys,
unmarked cemeteries. Billboards
are nothing but metal skeletons hiding
behind the clash of colors on tarpaulin.
The promise of whiter skin looms
over the patchwork maze of shacks.

No one mends a bullet-ridden car.
It becomes fodder to the crunching jaws
of scrap machinery, not a piece of evidence.

Who will remember those injured
in the night, the disappeared?
Are we only here to scavenge
a landscape where smoke coils
long after the last burning?

# And You Ring the Night

You hold a phone, though it is a banana
in the eyes of those who cannot see.
You cradle it from another time,
the rubber-covered wire
coiled around your arm again.

Outside it is late afternoon,
but your voice bears
the sleepless weight of dawn.

It is September, the season
to remember the disappeared.
And you ring the night watchman
who doesn't pick up. Your finger
makes precise movements
in the air; the rotary phone
spins back in silence.

# And You're in the Night

Sleep, a beast no chain could hold.
The bed misshapen by restless tossing,
as if I were wearing someone else's skin.
The flight of a bat that has lost its senses
in the dark, codes scrambled upon returning.

The spines of books I gave you grow fur
of dust. Words pressed against each other,
the leaves in no danger of causing papercuts.

And you're in the night, wandering
among memories, rooms with windows
bolted by brittle vines.

# End During the Night

No one ever told her it would somehow end
during the night. She just knew and expected it.
The same logic follows why she believes
the watches she stole (or borrowed)
and buried in shallow graves as a child
would never be found. In time,
she thought she, too, would look for them,
be lost and forgotten.

How could I ever hope
to change her, to make her feel
the warmth on the windowsill?
I tell her I was taught to rise
before dawn, before the rest of the city
crowded into jeeps and collectively inhaled
diesel fumes without the slightest resistance.
We all came home with layers
of soot on our skins.

I look for the sun even on overcast days.
She, the shadows long before nightfall.
Somehow we keep finding each other. Still.

# And During the Night

When the leopard frogs were roused from ground
that for years looked like cracked concrete,
the weight on the silenced highway was lifted
croak by croak, faint at first and few.

It must have taken time for the wet winter
to reach their secret place of slumber. As their bodies
wakened to the touch of water, their tongues,
instructed by instinct, stretched to caress eyes,
backs, limbs, bellies. Sacrificing sleep, I listened.

# Acknowledgments & Some Notes

"My Mother had a Concrete Garden" won the Magdala Award at the 2021 Poetry in McGregor Festival.

"Light and Rain" first appeared in the Clemengold anthology *Citrus Inspired Word Art.*

"Ant Garden" first appeared on the *AVBOB Poetry* website.

"The World is Round as a Drop of Water," "For Maria Ressa," and "After Seeing *Mad Max: Fury Road*" first appeared in the *Philippines Graphic Reader.*

"Light Attaches to a Girl," "Amorsolo's 'Tinikling in Barrio,'" and "Lecaroz's 'Bamboo Dancing'" first appeared in the monographs accompanying the art exhibits of Celeste Lecaroz.

"We Danced with Strangers" and "Dancing with a Phantom Limb" first appeared in *Hotazel Review.*

"For the Saviours" and "No Past, No Future" are translations of my own poem from the Filipino. They first appeared on the *Asymptote* website as part of their "Translation Tuesday" feature.

"Photograph in the Rain" in this book is different from the one first published in the book by Professor Ed Garcia, *Servant Leader: Leni Robredo.* This version is less historically accurate, but I believe it to be a better poem.

The quote from "The Soft Criminal" comes from an online pronouncement by former South African president Jacob Zuma, who has been accused of massive corruption during his reign. Here is a link: https://ewn.co.za/video/12520/zuma--the-law-is -too-soft-on-criminals.

"Discord" was first published in the *Ake Review*.

The quoted text in "Kaze No Denwa" comes from the article "Wind Phone" from *Atlas Obscura*, https://www.atlasobscura.com/places /wind-telephone.

"And During the Night" won first prize at the 2022 Poetry in McGregor Competition.

# About the Author

© Ken Barris

JIM PASCUAL AGUSTIN grew up in the Philippines during the Marcos dictatorship. He writes in Filipino and English. He holds a degree in English Literature from Ateneo de Manila University in the Philippines. He has been a lecturer, an NGO worker, a secondhand music shop employee, and a fridge cleaning kit seller, among others.

Agustin has published several books of poetry and a collection of stories in the Philippines, the UK, and South Africa. His poetry has won prizes in South Africa at the New Coin DALRO Awards, the EU Sol Plaatje Poetry Awards, the AVBOB Poetry Competition, and the Poetry in McGregor Competition. Lunch Ticket, a US-based online journal, awarded him the Gabo Prize.

He moved to Cape Town, South Africa in 1994 to be with the woman he fell in love with the year before while exploring the Mountain Province in the north of the Philippines during the monsoon season.

# About Gaudy Boy

From the Latin *gaudium*, meaning "joy," Gaudy Boy publishes books that delight readers with the various powers of art. The name is taken from the poem "Gaudy Turnout," by Singaporean poet Arthur Yap, about his time abroad in Leeds, the United Kingdom. Similarly inspired by such diasporic wanderings and migrations, Gaudy Boy brings literary works by authors of Asian heritage to the attention of an American audience and beyond. Established in 2018 as the imprint of the New York City–based literary nonprofit Singapore Unbound, we publish poetry, fiction, and literary nonfiction. Visit our website at www.singaporeunbound.org/gaudyboy.

## Previous Winners of the Gaudy Boy Poetry Book Prize
*Time Regime*, by Jhani Randhawa
*Object Permanence*, by Nica Bengzon
*Play for Time*, by Paula Mendoza
*Autobiography of Horse*, by Jenifer Sang Eun Park
*The Experiment of the Tropics*, by Lawrence Lacambra Ypil

## Fiction and Nonfiction
*Picking Off New Shoots Will Not Stop the Spring*, edited by Ko Ko Thett and Brian Haman
*The Infinite Library and Other Stories*, by Victor Fernando R. Ocampo
*The Sweetest Fruits*, by Monique Truong
*And the Walls Come Crumbling Down*, by Tania De Rozario
*The Foley Artist*, by Ricco Villanueva Siasoco
*Malay Sketches*, by Alfian Sa'at

## From Gaudy Boy Translates
*Amanat*, edited by Zaure Batayeva and Shelley Fairweather-Vega
*Ulirát*, edited by Tilde Acuña, John Bengan, Daryll Delgado, Amado Anthony G. Mendoza III, and Kristine Ong Muslim

CPSIA information can be obtained
at www.ICGtesting.com
Printed in the USA
BVHW032019170323
660681BV00004B/87

9 781958 652008